Through My Mind

Keetha Johnson

BookLeaf Publishing

Presentation by *BookLeaf Publishing*

Web: www.bookleafpub.com

E-mail: info@bookleafpub.com

ISBN: 978-93-95755-84-9

First edition 2022

DEDICATION

I would like to dedicate this collection of poems to the people who inspired them. With all due respect;

To some, thank you.

To others, fuck you.

ACKNOWLEDGEMENT

I would like to thank Bookleaf for making this (and my other 2 books) possible. Thank you for letting me live my dream!

As always, I would also like to thank all those who love and support me. I couldn't do what I do without you.

PREFACE

Writing is a wonderful coping mechanism, and through this collection of poems you will get a glimpse into the emotions and thoughts that may run through my mind at any given time. The heartbreak, grief, joy, or pure rage that I experience contribute to every single piece I write, with some of these poems being among my most personal.

#1

I hope you get all you've ever wanted
And it's not all that you'd hoped
I hope it's all that you deserve
For all the smoke you've blown

For every lie that's left your lips
For every knife in someone's back
For each time you hid your selfishness
With your "kind and caring" act

I can't help but wish for you
To get tangled in your web
Devoured by the anger
Of everyone that you mislead

And when your crimes begin to surface
And illuminate the truth
I hope you know that your undoing
Is on no one else but you.

#2

Your words have no foundation
Yet still are taken to be truth
You twist the situation
To make sure it suits you

Ruthless and unyielding
You'll push them past the edge
Nice words with condescending tone
You get in inside their head

You sweet talk and manipulate
Make it seem you're what you're not
Toss others underneath the bus
Without a second thought

So long as you come out on top
The ends justify the means
But no matter how you come across
Things are not always what they seem.

#3

Everytime I close my eyes
I can't help but see your face
And if love could have kept you here
I know you would have stayed

It comes in waves and I can't breathe
My heart stops in my chest
I'm sorry that I let you down
Wish I did more than my best

Each time the room falls silent
I wait to hear your call
To hear you crying out to us
While running down the hall

I hope that you rest easy
Knowing how loved you are
And even though you can't be here
I know you're never far.

#4

The fucking world is ending
And nobody noticed
So many distractions
We can't seem to focus

Who wore it better
Who committed what crime
Who knocked who up
While we run out of time

Irreparable damage
Done by the lot
So far passed FUBAR
Small attempts are for naught

No warm white light waiting
At the end of the tunnel
Just darkness and ash
While we claw through the rubble

Humans are flawed
Broken even in theory
So much so that
Of ourselves we are weary

Dishonest, disloyal,
And selfish to boot
Psychotic and violent
Bringing death over disputes

Minimal thinking
Content to destroy
Issues swept under the rug
Beneath our decoys

When will we wake up
Bring light to the end
Admit our mistakes
And stop playing pretend?

#5

Not a good night's sleep
Or a day without sorrow
Always wanting and hoping
For a better tomorrow

But a better tomorrow
Is far too elusive
And the main reason why
Remains inconclusive

Each day it changes
It's something new
Makes little difference
If it's lies or it's truth

Now it seems everything
Is so badly skewed
It's hard to see passed it
And know what to do

How to fix what's been broken
And battered and bruised
Put myself back together
After dealing with you.

#6

Can you finally see
All the damage that you've done
All the suffering you've caused
That you're not the only one

Not the only one
Whose chest aches when they breathe
Whose eyelids flash with nightmares
When they close their eyes to sleep

So many restless nights
Brought on by your pride
So many years spent running
From the pain and fear inside

Someday it'll catch you
You'll feel the weight of all you've done
And see how you became the darkness
By trying to be the sun.

#7

Everyone's concerned
With other's thoughts
As if they make a difference

It's like we think
They have the power
To diminish our magnificence

It's clichè to say
We burn bright regardless
Their hate can give us strength or weakness

It's us that choose
Which way it goes
If it gives us power or curses us with meekness

So make the choice
To stand your ground
Don't ever let them see your defenses fall

Keep pushing
Someday it'll change
You'll make it through and burn brighter than
them all.

#8

There's something so painful
About the gnawing in your stomach
Watching your dreams be experienced
By some other dumbfuck

All the plans you have in life
Feel the fire burning hot beneath your ass
You always thought if you believed
All your hopes would come to pass

But instead you sit there crying
On your kitchen floor
Wondering how you got here
When you know you deserve more

"Good things come to those who wait"
I've never heard such bullshit
There's wool over your eyes
And you're the one who pulled it

The ache in your chest won't subside
You think your meant for something bigger
Your ambition is a loaded gun
Man up and pull the trigger

Wipe the tears from your eyes
Get off your ass and move
If you won't do the work
Things will never improve

Stop waiting for the break you want
To fall into your lap
Go out and pave your own way
Work to close the gap

Between what you want and what you have
Where you are and want to be
Put in your time and pay your dues
Remember nothing comes for free.

#9

You think you've got us fooled
Like no one is the wiser
Trying to seem genuine
To become a trusted advisor

So you can manipulate the system
So you can rig the game
Dig your heels in deep
Plant your flag and stake your claim

Pull the strings and make believe
Play the victim when it suits you
Strong and confident 'til questioned
Then you appear to break in two

Forced sympathy is unbecoming
And easy to see through
I don't want your sympathy or "help"
If it's any less than true

So mind your own and watch your ass
Because the truth will set us free
And you'll feel each one leave you behind
I hope it brings you to your knees.

#10

Why do you let them
Take without giving
How are you content
Surviving not living

You continue to let them
Darken your light
You seem so beaten down
Left with no fight

You're worth so much more
Than they make you believe
They kill pieces of you
And won't allow you to grieve

You deserve so much more
Than what you get stuck with
Too tired to notice
Just how much you miss

I wish you could see you
In the same light that I do
See all the wonder
In everything you do

I hope you find freedom
I wish you true love
I hope you can heal
And when push comes to shove

I hope you know that you're welcome
And that no matter what
My door will always be open
When all others are shut.

#11

Does It make you feel good
To take what isn't yours
Does it make you feel strong
Each time you slam a door

Do you believe it's better
To be not loved but feared
Does it give you satisfaction
To be the cause of tears

Do you take swings without intention
Or do you set out to maim
Wear their bruises like medals
Make sure they remember your name

Do you leave because you like the chase
Like to make them think it's over
Move from one onto the next
Or herd them like sheep to a drover

And have a multitude to choose from
To fulfill your every want
Break them and forget them
Without a second thought

Someday they'll see the real you
And find solace in the truth
That you're weak and you're pathetic
That they deserve more than your abuse

You're insecure, inconsequential
Useless and unhinged
They'll burn you straight to the ground
To little more than ashes in the wind.

#12

I may be a selfish person
About that there is no doubt
But if I have the means to
I'm always happy to help out

So say what you want about me
But we all have our sins
Can you own your vices
Admit to where you've been

Can you be a book so open
Your pages crystal clear
Can you own each of your mistakes
Or do you live in fear

Of how people will perceive you
Should they get a glimpse behind the mask
Can you display your failures with pride
With dignity and class

See I've learned from my choices
Be them bad or good
And I fight everyday
To live life as I should

So maybe you should clean your stoep
Before you try to dirty mine
'Cause I've made peace with all my flaws
And I'm gonna be just fine.

#13

My skin is stretched and blemished
My weight higher than it should be
Crooked teeth and glasses
Yet unapologetically just me

My hair may not fall how I want it
Bags caress the bottoms of my eyes
I may not have the body of a model
But the one I have suits me just fine

They say beauty's on the inside
Personality's what counts
But I believe that's bullshit
And it's time we figured out

The truth about how beauty lies
In the eyes of the beholder
So don't take that cliche line to heart
Don't let your fire merely smolder

Let it burn their fucking house down
While you dance among the flames
Let yourself be lead by confidence
Don't let them forget your name.

#14

I can never seem to find
The words needed to describe
The things you do to me
The way you make me feel inside

The warmth each time I see you
That creeps up from my toes
And the softness of your touch
As though caressed by a rose

And how the fluttering that starts out small
Like petals gliding on a breeze
Quickly becomes so overwhelming
It could bring me to my knees

I've never felt this strongly
Or had it last this long
I thought love was make believe
But I'm so glad I was wrong.

#15

We both know that smile
That seems so genuine is fake
And although you hide it well
You're a fucking snake

Pathetic and deplorable
Somehow you still think you're a hero
Think you're the sun, the moon, the stars
But you're nothing but a zero

The lies you tell are aging
Your rope is coming to an end
In time all truths will surface
Your reign is up, my friend.

#16

What makes you so special
That you think you have the right to brag
When you're simply ordinary
Held together by red flags

You think you've been so charming
But the walls have ears and eyes
They hear every word you say
They see right through your lies

Everyone can see you
For what you really are
You read just like a children's book
It really isn't hard

You bite the hands that feed you
Seem to think you're silver-tongued
And that misguided confidence
Will be the reason you're undone.

#17

How can you be so stupid
Not see the mistakes you make
Express that you have nothing left
And still you let them take

Makeup covers bruises
Shades cover up black eyes
But you know now who they really are
So why does it come as a surprise

When they raise their voice to you
Or even worse, their fists
Why do you lay down and take it
When you should be getting pissed

When you should be packing up your shit
And never looking back
Clearly common sense
Has become something that you lack

But you need to open your eyes
Think with your head and not your heart
Cut ties with these assholes
Before they tear you apart.

#18

What are you thinking
Where the hell is your brain
Say you want it to change
But let it stay the same

You're strong but still human
Can't say the same about them
Losers and psychos
Pathetic wannabe men

Little boys with huge egos
No fear of you leaving
Are only enabled
By your self-deceiving

Belief that they love you
Or that they'll change
After all that they've done
You must be derranged

To think that there's even
A small chance in hell
That they'll get better
That they'll treat you well

Please give up the delusions
Cut the shit and cut ties
Kick them to the curb
While you're still alive

You've got to get out
Before it's too late
Ask yourself, truly
How much more can you take?

#19

Hold me down
Steal the air
Directly from my lungs

Bruise my eyes
Abuse my thighs
Convince me that we're just having fun

Lie to me
Make me think
I'm your one and only

Then walk away
Leave me to die
But come back when you get lonely

Pick me up
And play with me
Like I'm your favourite toy

Break me down
Cast me aside
Once I'm finally destroyed

Take all that
I have to give
Leave me with nothing left

Still I yearn
For your return
As if I am possessed

There's no escape
I'm in too deep
It seems you've dug my grave

I guess I'm stuck
Shit out of luck
Forever as your slave.

#20

Do you hear yourself talk
Even know what you're saying
Or do you just like the sound of your voice

Do your words have meaning
Any substance at all
Or are they just senseless noise

Do you notice how often
You interrupt others
Or do you think you're too important to care

Is it important to you
To have an audience
Or do you still talk when no one is there

Have you ever given
Even one single thought
To someone outside of yourself

Maybe you should
Before it's too late
And you're left alone with no one to help.

#21

What are we doing
And how did we get here
Surviving each day
Living in fear

Will it be the climate
The virus, the sun
Or will the greed and the weapons
Leave us undone

Will we kill the planet
Or will it kill us first
Each hurdle we conquer
Leads to something worse

So will it be cosmic
Or just human disdain
That kills us slowly
Until nothing remains?